December 24, 1987

For Pat, with love at
Christmas, and for always,

Christiana

The Fireside Book

A picture and a poem
for every mood
chosen by

David Hope

Printed and Published by
D. C. THOMSON & CO., LTD.,
185 Fleet Street, London EC4A 2HS.
ISBN 0 85116 405 6
© D. C. Thomson & Co., Ltd., 1987

THE WORLD'S MUSIC

I WAKEN when the morning's come,
  And feel the air and light alive
With strange sweet music like the hum
  Of bees about their busy hive.

The linnets play among the leaves
  At hide-and-seek, and chirp and sing;
While, flashing to and from the eaves,
  The swallows twitter on the wing.

And twigs that shake, and boughs that sway,
  And tall old trees you could not climb,
And winds that come, but cannot stay,
  Are singing gaily all the time.

From dawn to dark the old mill-wheel
  Makes music, going round and round;
And dusty-white with flour and meal,
  The miller whistles to its sound.

The brook that flows beside the mill,
  As happy as a brook can be,
Goes singing its own song until
  It learns the singing of the sea.

For every wave upon the sands
  Sings songs you never tire to hear,
Of laden ships from sunny lands
  Where it is summer all the year.

The coals beneath the kettle croon,
  And clap their hands and dance in glee;
And even the kettle hums a tune
  To tell you when it's time for tea.

Gabriel Setoun

THE LINNET

THE purple shadows darken down the sky:
  Across the fields the bell of evening rings;
Yet over by the wood a linnet sings,
  Pouring her soul in song to God on high.

So would I send my song to Him, the giver
  Of wooded glen and tumbling mountain
    stream;
Of dew-drenched flower and wide, deep-
    flowing river,
  And linnets singing in the Vales of Dream.

Sleep, crimson rose . . .
  Sleep, gentle honeysuckle,
Thy fragrance lingering the leaves among:
  Sleep, golden bird, while memory recaptures
The magic cadence of thy heavenly song.

Sydney Bell

TEN

TEN is very big by day,
   When other boys are there;
Oh, heavy boots and manly tread,
And ready fists and tousled head,
And talks of games and noisy shout,
When other chaps are round about—
Then Ten is my despair.

But Ten is very small at night,
I thank the powers that be;
A rosy cheek and soft brown head
He burrows in his little bed;
And pillowed there, with his warmth warm,
A soldier doll sleeps on his arm;
Pathetic now the thin brown fist,
And Ten, at night, likes to be kissed,
And Ten belongs to me.

Mabel V. Irvine

I WENT down to Grindleford
   In the Springtime and the rain.
There the woodland glistened green,
    Glistened green the sprouting grain,
Round about the frowning hills
   Bearing clouds of sombre hue,
Till anon the raindrops ceased
   And the sun came shyly through.

Then the gloomy Millstone Edge
   Ceased to frown and smiled at me.
Came the gentle coaxing breeze
   Murmured, " Come! Oh come and see!
See the babbling stream below;
   Climb the rocky wooded slope,
Watch the sluggish local train
   Gliding down the vale to Hope."

Stately beech and slender birch
   Formed an archway overhead,
As I sauntered through the glade
   By the path which upwards led
Till I reached the bouldered heath
   And the vantage point Surprise,
Where the sweep of hill and dale
   Leaps in glory to the eyes.

That was very long ago,
   —Sterner calls have breached my day—
Yet the lure of hill and dale
   Beckons me from work away;
And the time can't come too soon
   When I'll take the road again
Swinging out to Grindleford
   In the Springtime and the rain.

J. P. Huston

A CLOTHES LINE

I SAW a song swing
  Between two apple-trees,
A gay song fluttering
In the sun-warmed breeze,
In high tones of white joy,
And deep tones of blue,
And tender tones of violet,
A scale of merry hue.

Such a happy song,
Swinging on a line
Between two apple-trees,
In the sunshine!

Florence Irene Gubbins

A CAT

OUR terriers sit with restless ear and eye,
  Waiting to follow where the Master goes;
They have a notion where a walk will lie,
  But Pussy knows.

Remote, inscrutable, a cryptic power,
  Like Egypt's cat-god with the emerald eyes,
Wrapped in herself she waits upon her hour,
  Then off she hies.

Down the white steps you see her shadow creep,
  Across the lawn, and through the low beech
    hedge,
Then up the high fence darts, a monstrous leap,
  And holds its edge.

Now down into the long, lush grass she drops,
  Congenial jungle for her soul to range,
As did her ancestors the mountain tops;
  She does not change;

Untamed inheritor of ages dim,
  A silken courtier but a killer dire,
At breakfast-time you'll find her washed and prim
  Before the fire.

H. R. Pyatt

IDYLL

LITTLE Jenny Linden,
  Tripping down the street,
Golden leaves of autumn
  All about your feet,
Swallows flying southward
  Through the glowing skies,
Little imps of mischief
  Dancing in your eyes.

Little Jenny Linden,
  Standing by the stream,
Mirrored by the water,
  Captured by a dream,
Wanton evening breezes
  Toying with your hair,
Playing on my heart-strings:
  Jenny, do you care?

Little Jenny Linden,
  There's a moon above;
Have you done with waiting?
  Won't you fall in love?
Youth's the time for courting;
  'Tis folly to delay!
I would have no other;
  Answer me today.

Little Jenny Linden,
  The moon is very bright;
Say you'll love me always,
  As you do tonight.
When the Spring, returning,
  Bursts the buds of May,
We shall stand together
  On our wedding day.

                    Peter Cliffe

THE CANOE SPEAKS

ON the great streams the ships may go
    About men's business to and fro.
But I, the egg-shell pinnace, sleep
On crystal waters ankle-deep:
I, whose diminutive design,
Of sweeter cedar, pithier pine,
Is fashioned on so frail a mould,
A hand may launch, a hand withhold:
I, rather, with the leaping trout,
Wind, among lilies, in and out;
I, the unnamed, inviolate,
Green, rustic rivers, navigate;
My dipping paddle scarcely shakes
The berry in the bramble-brakes;
Still forth on my green way I wend
Beside the cottage garden-end;
And by the nested angler fare,
I take the lovers unaware.
By willow wood and water-wheel
Speedily fleets my touching keel;
By all retired and shady spots
Where prosper dim forget-me-nots.

Robert Louis Stevenson

THE WEAVER OF DREAMS

I WEAVE my dreams, but no one sees;
   They are so fine and fair;
Alone, and sheltered by the trees
I weave my dreams, but no one sees,
   For dreams are made of air.

I weave my dreams, but no one knows;
   They only smile and say,
" How very old and wise she grows;
She thinks of fairies, I suppose . . .
   Her thoughts are miles away."

I weave my dreams, but who can see
   Their gold and silver gleams?
These airy thoughts that come to me
Are mine to treasure secretly . . .
   I cannot share my dreams.

Gloria Rawlinson

BOWLING

HERE'S a song we all can sing,
   With the blue sky o'er us;
Old and young, in every tongue,
   Join us in the chorus.
Cricket from its perch may fall,
   Football leaves us scowling;
But the game to beat them all—
   Good old game of bowling!

Games can come, and games can go,
    Bowling lasts for ever;
Friendships made, that bowls have laid,
    Death can only sever.
Here's a green, that's fast and keen,
    Here's a shot that's glorious;
Kiss the Jack, and run her back,
    And leave the rink victorious.

Round about the festive board,
    Old opponents mingle;
Once again, to play the game,
    While the glasses jingle.
In defeat, we'll own we're beat—
    Take it without howling;
When we win, we'll shout "Chin Chin!"
    Good old game of bowling.

William Neish

THE PLOUGHMAN

UNDER the long fell's stony eaves
    The ploughman, going up and down,
Ridge after ridge man's tide-mark leaves,
    And turns the hard grey soil to brown.

Striding, he measures out the earth
    In lines of life, to rain and sun;
And every year that comes to birth
    Sees him striding on and on.

The seasons change, and then return;
    Yet still, in blind, unsparing ways,
However I may shrink or yearn,
    The ploughman measures out my days.

His acre brought forth roots last year;
    This year it bears the gloomy grain;
Next Spring shall seedling grass appear;
    Then roots and corn and grass again.

Five times the young corn's pallid green
    I have seen spread and change and thrill;
Five times the reapers I have seen
    Go creeping up the far-off hill:

And, as the unknowing ploughman climbs
    Slowly and inveterately,
I wonder long how many times
    The corn will spring again for me.

Gordon Bottomley

THE LITTLE RATH

QUIET lies gently over the little rath,
   The quiet of ages that settled long ago
When the last dweller turned at the edge of the
      road
And looked for a moment before his footsteps died
Away in the mist, and silence fell over the field.

Quiet lies gently over the little rath;
Nobody knows its name or will ever know
Who were the builders. Only the wandering winds
Could tell whose the voices that whisper out of the
        past;
Could tell why the sudden laughter; the heartfelt
sigh.

Quiet lies gently over the little rath.

Sydney Bell

FAIRY MUSIC

WHEN the fiddlers play their tunes you may sometimes hear,
Very softly chiming in, magically clear,
Magically high and sweet, the tiny crystal notes
Of fairy voices bubbling free from tiny fairy throats.

When the birds at break of day chant their
    morning prayers,
Or on sunny afternoons pipe ecstatic airs,
Comes an added rush of sound to the silver
    din—
Songs of fairy troubadours gaily joining in.

When athwart the drowsy fields summer twilight
    falls,
Through the tranquil air there float elfin madrigals,
And in wild November nights, on the winds astride,
Fairy hosts go rushing by, singing as they ride.

Every dream that mortals dream, sleeping or
    awake,
Every lovely fragile hope—these the fairies take,
Delicately fashion them and give them back again
In tender, limpid melodies that charm the hearts
    of men.

Rose Fyleman

AH! WESTMINSTER

ONCE on a sunny morning
  By Westminster way I went,
For I would see Westminster
  Ere all my days were spent.

Full fifty fateful summers
  Had passed o'er my vacant head —
I'd never seen Westminster
  And soon I would be dead.

Westminster — it is famous
  Wherever free men go;
It stands because, God willing,
  The English made it so.

I entered by St Stephen's —
  The ancient Hall and Gate —
And marvelled at its story
  From days that know no date.

Up steps into the Chamber,
  Where Lords and Commons meet —
I saw the Speaker passing —
  I! A mere man from the street!

And when I left and took my way,
  I crossed Westminster Hall —
A resolution now fulfilled,
  For I had seen it all.

Now I can go and live or die —
  It doesn't matter much!
I've been and seen Westminster
  And there's none other such.

                    William Darling

PANSIES

WHEN the shamed sun westward flies,
 Routed by the gloaming hour,
And the victor's shadow lies
 Cool on each heat-weary flower,
In my pleasant pansy row
 Blue and golden heads droop low.

Water-freshened, watch them raise
 Wet bright faces gratefully,
While the mounting fragrance says
 Pansies' grace of thanks to me;
Night's grey wing wafts breezes cold,
 Gaily dance my blue and gold.

So when a smiling hill and sea,
 On a sunny holiday,
Shower on toilers bounteously
 Gifts of joy and healing play,
Each tired body, weary brain,
 Glad, refreshed, looks up again.

While from countless happy hearts
 Rises, all unconsciously,
Fragrance, joy-distilled, and starts
 Mist-like upward to the sky.
Sweeter than my flowers to me
 Grace of joy to heaven must be.

Hylda C. Cole

EARLY MARCH

I DO not see her anywhere
  (Yet she is fair!)
I hear her laughter flowing
    And know her growing
In crimsoning hedgerows where
A thrush is singing on a bare
    Bright branch. O dear
She is in her invisible brightness!
    And not too soon
Would I behold her whiteness
    In beauty's blossoming.

She has kissed the furrowed fields
    that lie
    Under a sky
All white-embroidered where
Sunbeams in bright gleams
Ruby the berried hedge. Ah there
    Her feet have lingered
    And the air
Is soft with her sweet odours. Fair
Is she in her invisible brightness,
    And not too soon
Would I behold her whiteness
    In beauty's blossoming.

Florence Irene Gubbins

THE DESERTED GARDEN

NOW they are gone, these beautiful playfellows,
   Gone from the green lawns under my
   balcony,
Gone—and the house no more, the orchard
Echoes no more to their happy laughter.

How oft I watched them playing, the innocent
Boy friend and girl friend under the cedar-tree,
Till through the soft dusk rose the twinkling
Stars, and the lamps in the lane were shining.

Fair head to dark head, leaning and whispering,
Old games and new games, pirates and Indians,
Short skirts and bare knees madly racing,
Climbing aloft on the cedar branches.

Day comes and night comes, summer and holiday,
Swift ah! the bright hours, merry adventurers!
Tears now, a first shy kiss at parting,
Tears and a hand at the corner waving.

White through the dawn-mist, careless of
   yesterdays,
Life stretches onward, life the attainable
White road along dim hills of dreamland;
Childhood is dead, and the leaves drift over.

Yet here in bleak house slumbers the memory,
Here, here, in green lawn, orchard and cedar-tree,
Fair head and dark head, laughter, laughter,
Evening and voices across the starlight.

P. Hugh B. Lyon

A SONG OF BENDISH

SUCH lazy miles to Bendish!
  Past banks whereon the Queen Anne's lace
Grows tall enough to brush the face;
It's best to choose a gentle pace
If you would go to Bendish.

Such winding miles to Bendish!
The road's as narrow as a stream,
All dappled shadow, golden gleam,
And gates by which to stand and dream:
Why hasten on to Bendish?

Such sleepy miles to Bendish!
Sleek cattle drowsing 'neath the trees,
A summer sound like distant seas,
Where leaves are crooning to the breeze
A lullaby of Bendish.

Such happy miles to Bendish!
Long-cherished scenes round every bend;
A little gossip with a friend;
A cottage small at journey's end;
And love and peace in Bendish.

Peter Cliffe

THE SPELL

BEFORE the night was cloven
  Or morning's spears aflame,
I knew the spell was woven
  To bind the day that came:

It seemed the great earth trembled,
  The wind was strange and shy,
The ancient seas dissembled
  Their lone and boding cry;

And, as the sap that rises
  Disturbs the heart of Spring,
The sense of near surprises
  Made all my pulses sing.

Blind hope and phantom warning
  Are vaguely touched with fire—
My heart has faced the morning,
  Desiring to desire!

And now the hills have framed you,
  Advancing careless yet,
And now my lips have named you,
  And now my hands have met.

Oh, light of eyes uplifted!
  Oh, pang of love begun!
Our wandering lives have drifted
  How strangely into one!

Gerald Gould

UNTO THE HILLS

OH, there's trouble in the valley
    There's sorrow in the street,
And all the ways are saddened there
    With heavy-going feet.

But up upon the mountain-top,
    Away from town or street,
The only tears are on the grass,
    With heart's-ease at your feet;
And just the fleecy sheep are there
    With climbing steps so fleet.

Oh, there's trouble in the valley,
   There's sorrow in the street,
And all the ways are saddened there
   With heavy-going feet.

But up upon the mountain-top,
   Away from town or street,
The sunbeams smile above your head,
   There's greenness at your feet,
And clouds go scuddling down below,
   With wild birds wheeling fleet;
While in the little wind's caress
   The kiss of heaven you meet!

Morag Bell

THE LITTLE HOMES

MY heart goes out to the little homes
   That star the mountains high,
Where the cloud swirls down when the sun
   goes in,
  And the blue smoke greets the sky;
With their snug brown thatch, and the low half
   door
  Where the wide-eyed children play,
And the welcome light in the window waits
  For the Ones who went away.

The sea lies calm when the dawn light
  Comes creeping down the hill,
When the larks rise high in the pearly sky
  And the morning air is chill;
Then the mother kneels and stirs to flame
  The smould'ring peats o' grey
That light her eyes as she breathes a prayer
  For the Ones who went away.

Oh dear to me are the dark hills,
  As dear the dewy glen
When the blackthorn tree is a joy to see
  And the whins are gold again.
But my heart goes out to the little homes
  Below the rocks o' grey,
Where still the light in the window waits
  For the Ones who went away.

Sydney Bell

HOME THOUGHTS

BLACKBIRD on the hawthorn bough
 Is looking in at me.
He wonders why I linger now
When there's so much to see.
Back home the cowslips are in bloom;
No chaffinch sings in this dull room.

So it's farewell to Telex clack
And goodbye to the phone.
Tomorrow I am going back
To that small plot I own.
Above it plovers wheel and cry,
And there are miles and miles of sky.

I'll never be a wealthy man,
Or even well-to-do.
The challenge of the forward plan
I'd rather leave to you.
But though I'll own no private plane,
I'll be a man who's home again.

Peter Cliffe

ESSEX FLOWER-WAYS

I LONG for Essex in Springtime,
  Blue violets hiding shy
'Neath crimson-tufted larches
  In a copse where the road winds high.
Oh, for Howe Wood with its bluebells,
  Where azure carpets lie
Dotted with cowslips freckled,
  Say, what with their scent can vie?
I long for great fields of poppies
  'Mid wheat and barley and rye,
All tawny and scarlet in sunshine,
  As I thread their tall growth by.
I want green shade of the Beech Walk,
  Its silvery trunks to spy,
With boughs like cathedral arches,
  Field temples beneath God's sky!
Oh! give me the frail blue harebells,
  Climbing the chalk-banks high,
Where tangled clematis riots
  And binds with its silver tie!
The rose and orange of spindle,
  With scarlet berries vie,
And golden glories of beechwoods
  Flame 'neath an autumn sky!
Oh! I starve for the Essex flower-ways,
  Their myriad beauties cry,
"Come, where you used to wander,
  Joy in your heart and eye."

Mary Bell

THE HERON

HIS haunts are by the shallow strands
    of unfrequented streams;
Behold, on stilt-like legs he stands
    And with hunched shoulders dreams.

His image, mirrored at his feet,
    By rippling waters blurr'd,
Shows him aloof, reserved, discreet,
    A melancholy bird.

This solitary misanthrope
    A silent vigil keeps;
But now he has abandoned hope,
    He watches not, but sleeps.

He stands as stiffly as a log,
    He blinks but once or twice—
Out shoots his neck, a wriggling frog,
    Is swallowed in a trice.

W. D. Cocker

THE CHILD NEXT DOOR

THE child next door has a wreath on her hat,
　　Her afternoon frock sticks out like that,
　　　　　　All soft and frilly;
She doesn't believe in fairies at all
(She told me over the garden wall)—
　　　　　　She thinks they're silly.

The child next door has a watch of her own,
She has shiny hair and her name is Joan
　　　　　　(Mine's only Mary),
But doesn't it seem very sad to you
To think that she never her whole life through
　　　　　　Has seen a fairy?

Rose Fyleman

SNOW

LOVELIER than words can paint,
  Frail beyond compare,
Lifeless, chill and colourless,
  Drifting through the air;
At a single touch dissolved
  On its journey slow,
What could be more impotent
  Than a flake of snow?

Soft, yet irresistible,
  White, with steely blue
Shadows in its dazzling glare,
  Burying from view
Under its thick, icy pall
  All the summer's glow,
What could more relentless prove
  Than a mass of snow?

M. Austin Page

INVITATION

TWO hundred years
　My house has stood;
Its walls are thick,
　Its roof is good.

Not grand or small,
　Rambling or squat;
Nothing it should be
　It is not.

A yeoman's house,
　Light, kind and gay
Where burgesses
　Braved out their day.

Its gracious rooms
　Have just that air
Which bids you in
　And keeps you there.

They house my books,
　Long row on row,
And friendly chairs
　And fireside glow.

The garden walled,
　The cellars dry;
There burgundies
　And clarets lie.

Come then and taste
　Since years are few,
There is a room
　For friends, for you!

C. C. Abbott

JUNE

IF I should sleep through many moons and
   seasons,
   And then one morning waken from my dreaming
To find around me, glistening and gleaming,
   Ten thousand buttercups . . .

If in the hedge I found a wild rose twining
   And giant hollyhocks were climbing high,
If creamy-white syringa boughs were shining
   And swifts sped through the sky . . .

If in the grass I found a skylark nesting,
   And busy bees droned out their humdrum tune—
I should not need a calendar to tell me
   That it was glorious June!

Elsie S. Campbell

GOLDEN DANCING DAYS

THERE are fairy bells a-ringing,
   There is tinkle of a lute,
And the Piper comes a-singing,
   With his magic fairy flute.
Won't you listen, listen, listen
   To the melody he plays,
With the dew-drops all a-glisten
   In the golden dancing days!

Oh! the rapture and the laughter
   In the Piper's magic tone!
Leave your dreams and follow after
   Ere the dancing days are flown!

Don't you hear the music falling?
   Don't you hear the fairy feet?
Oh! the Piper, crooning, calling,
   Oh! the fluting silver-sweet!
Over hill and dale and hollow
   With his tripping train he strays,
Won't you follow, follow, follow
   In the golden dancing days!

Won't you join the fun and laughter
   While the Piper still is nigh,
Ere the Winter follows after
   And the dancing days go by!

                              Anne Page

EVENING IN WHITEPARK BAY

DOWN along the level sands the tiny waves are
    creeping,
  Leaving frothy fingers as they turn and race
    away;
Out beyond the hidden reefs the green-
    backed surf goes leaping,
  Booming low and distant in the silence of the
    bay.

Down among the shady dunes the silver gulls
    are dreaming,
  Standing white and ghostly with their breasts
    towards the sea;
Softly through their folded wings the twilight
    breezes, streaming,
  Ruffle silver feathers like the leaflets on the
    tree.

On the sandhills' moonlit brown the windswept
    sands are sifting;
  Only comes the murmur of the breakers far
    away;
Slowly down the summer sky the clouds of
    night go drifting:
  All is hushed and sleeping till the breaking of
    the day.

Sydney Bell

ON CHOSEN HILL

ON Chosen Hill, so long ago,
　　We strayed together, I and you,
With summer roses all a-blow,
　　When life was very fresh and new.
(Are sweet wild roses blowing still
　　On Chosen Hill, on Chosen Hill?)

Such years ago — so long, it seems —
　　We watched the fleeting shadows pass,
And heard the fairy flute of dreams
　　That whispered in the waving grass.
(Do little winds go sighing still
　　On Chosen Hill, on Chosen Hill?)

Ah, would the years but set me free,
　　It's I'd be going once again
Where buried lies the heart of me,
　　And I would climb the winding lane
To find the dreams that linger still
　　On Chosen Hill, on Chosen Hill!

Anne Page

CARGOES

QUINQUIREME of Nineveh, from distant Ophir,
   Rowing home to haven in sunny Palestine,
    With a cargo of ivory,
    And apes and peacocks,
Sandalwood, cedarwood, and sweet white wine.

Stately Spanish galleon coming from the Isthmus,
Dipping through the Tropics by the palm-green shores,
    With a cargo of diamonds.
    Emeralds, amethysts,
Topazes, and cinnamon, and gold moidores.

Dirty British coaster with a salt-caked smoke stack
Butting through the Channel in the mad March days,
    With a cargo of Tyne coal,
    Road rail, pig lead,
Firewood, ironware, and cheap tin trays.

John Masefield

THE ADVENTURE

LET us adventure;
  Stealthily, gently go forward
With hearts all a-trespassing
Into the high hill land.

Let us go softly;
The Wind with the Northern Streamers
Conjoins the black cloak of Night
With his unseen hand.

Let us not whisper;
Here where the pale bog-maidens
Rise up from the fallen stars
To die with the day.

Let us not linger;
The long white hair of the mist-man
Has tangled the moon's magic scent
To draw us away.

Could we not stay here?
To dance with the gay silver birches?
To walk with the great Grey Man
And his echo-lure?

O, let us return!
Though every step be a sorrow,
We have caught the longing which
No man's will can cure.

Wendy Wood

SEPTEMBER ENDS

SO now September ends; above the sea
  One drifting gull emits his plaintive cry,
Haunting, and keeping lonely watch with me,
Wheeling above the shadows from the sky.
Ours is a harmony of solitude,
Ours the soul-union, gotten without speech,
That shares and understands the heart's wild mood
When love has turned to jetsam of the beach:
For I am gone from you, am desolate.
He is bereft: his flock has winged away.
We are sad monarchs of a tide-bound state,
Without one subject in this dying day;
And ever on my ears (O serpent hiss!)
Surf brushes shingle with a lover's kiss.

John Gawsworth

APPLE-RINGIE*

THERE'S a wee old-fashioned garden
   That has haunted me for years;
I have seen it in my laughter,
   I can see it through my tears.
It boasts no tiger lilies,
   And it know no regal rose;
Just a sweet old-fashioned garden,
   Where the apple-ringie grows.

I can see its boxwood border,
   With a splash of London Pride,
While thyme and clove carnations
   Keep nodding side by side;
Verbena, musk, and hollyhocks,
   Their scented perfume throws,
About this old-world garden,
   Where the apple-ringie grows.

Far back along Time's roadway,
   In my happy boyhood hours,
I chased the sleepy bumble bees
   That landed on the flowers.
I wakened up the butterflies
   That seemed to seek repose,
Inside that rustic garden,
   Where the apple-ringie grows.

There's a dear old-fashioned garden,
   Far away on Scotia's plain,
And there's times when I keep longing
   Just to see it once again.
And this yearning gets the stronger,
   As Life's day draws to a close—
Just to see this bonnie garden,
   Where the apple-ringie grows.

William Neish

*Southernwood (Scots)

DE GUSTIBUS

I AM an unadventurous man,
  And always go upon the plan
Of shunning danger where I can.
And so I fail to understand
Why every year a stalwart band
Of tourists go to Switzerland,
And spend their time for several weeks,
With quaking hearts and pallid cheeks,
Scaling abrupt and windy peaks.
Some men pretend they think it bliss
To clamber up a precipice
Or dangle over an abyss,
To crawl along a mountain side,
Supported by a rope that's tied
—Not too securely to a guide;
But such pretences, it is clear,
In the aspiring mountaineer
Are usually insincere.
So I, for one, do not propose
To cool my comfortable toes
In regions of perpetual snows,
As long as I can take my ease,
Fanned by a soothing southern
breeze,
Under the shade of English trees.
And any one who leaves my share
Of English fields and English air
May take the Alps for aught I care!

St. John Hankin

MEMORY

As a perfume doth remain
    In the folds where it hath lain,
So the thought of you, remaining
Deeply folded in my brain,
Will not leave me: all things leave me:
You remain.

Other thoughts may come and go,
Other moments I may know
That shall waft me, in their going,
As a breath blown to and fro,
Fragrant memories: fragrant memories
Come and go.

Only thoughts of you remain
In my heart where they have lain,
Perfumed thoughts of you, remaining,
A hid sweetness, in my brain.
Others leave me: all things leave me:
You remain.

                              Arthur Symons

CASTLES ON THE SAND

TOWARD your fortress, bravely planned—
 Moat and bridge and towers and keep—
Little waves steal up the strand,
 Nearer creep and nearer creep;
Nobody can stop a tide;
 King Canute was told he could,
But he knew before he tried
 That it wasn't any good.

Now your moat is full of wet,
 Which is what a moat is for;
Now your tumbled ramparts get
 Badly mixed up with the floor;
But you chose this fatal site
 Knowing well you must be downed,
And you'll laugh with pure delight
 When the topmost tower is drowned.

Ah! but you who dare the sea,
 Who, with life still at the morn,
Better than a victory
 Love to lead a chance forlorn,
Will you, when you're not so small,
 Build, for safety, up the beach,
Where the tide, however tall,
 Isn't tall enough to reach?

Will you build on solid rock
 (This is much the best address),
Run no risk of any shock,
 Take the line of safe success?

Will you no more love to play
 Losing games? Why, so, my son,
You'll be following wisdom's way,
 But — it won't be half the fun!

Sir Owen Seaman

THE WISHING WELL

COME, let us to the Wishing Well,
 Deep hidden in the mossy dell,
Where water binds, as with a spell,
All those who would their wishes tell.

We'll watch the dragonflies display
Their rainbow hues, like jewelled spray,
And if a bright kingfisher darts
Then wonder will delight our hearts.

There in the water, gleaming, cool,
As our reflections fill the pool,
Deep in the Wishing Well we'll see
Two faces peering — you and me.

And when our coins we freely fling
We'll wish for almost anything,
For in the ripples, so it seems,
Our shining coins will mirror dreams.

Come, do not idle, no one tell,
Let's hurry to the Wishing Well,
And there we'll both together join,
To make a wish and toss a coin.

Glynfab John

DUSK

THE long day has ended,
   The sun has descended,
A red moon lifts over the hill.
The first stars are glancing,
The mayflies are dancing,
And the evening is solemn and still.

The church bells are ringing,
A sweet bird is singing,
A small bat flits over the sky.
A white owl goes sailing,
The soft light is failing,
A noisy, late tractor rolls by.

A cool breeze is sighing,
The pale moths are flying,
A splendour emblazons the west.
I'm done with my roaming
And now through the gloaming
I gladly go home to my rest.

Peter Cliffe

LENT LILIES

ALL the world has roses,
  And Summer joys to spare,
But we two kissed in Springtime,
  With incense in the air;
And they that weave their garlands,
  How should they understand
Why I bring only lilies,
  And lay them in your hand?

All the world has music,
  And nightingales to sing,
But blackbirds they were calling,
  When we two kissed in Spring.
Let all the world have roses,
  All birds but one be dumb,
But I will bring you lilies
  Till our Easter Morning come!

Anne Page

EAST AND WEST

THERE are wide white roads in the east land,
   They lead over weald and wold,
But the little brown lanes of the west land
   Are dear as a tale that is old.

The gay glad flowers of the east land,
   They flame on the broad highway,
Yet the little shy buds of the west land
   Are fairer to me than they.

There are broad barley fields in the east land,
    And acre on acre of rye,
But no kind little hedge, like the west land,
    For lone folks to wander by.

There's a shout in the wind of the east land,
    'Tis clean, and triumphant, and chill,
But a sigh in the wind from the west land
    Is calling, and calling me still.

Fay Inchfawn

THE MERRY HEART

OH! I'll take a merry heart
　　Along the road I go,
And I'll throw a merry laugh
　　To all the winds that blow!
And the sour winds that sweep the sky,
　　And beat across the sea,
Shall whistle to a cheery tune,
　　And laugh along with me.

Oh! I'll sing a merry song
　　Along the stony mile,
And I'll leave a merry laugh
　　Beside the awkward stile.
And the grey way shall wake again
　　To music and to laughter,
With milestones of cheery songs,
　　For the feet that follow after.

Oh! I'll keep a forward face,
　　And never look behind,
And I'll send the wistful thoughts
　　A-whistling down the wind.
And I'll only care to keep for mine,
　　Of all the road shall pay,
A last laugh in the long run,
　　And a good heart all the way.

Anne Page

LOVE'S CALENDAR

NOW is it Spring once more?
  Do bluebells line the lane,
And primroses a carpet make,
  Violets a mist like rain?
Is the wind cool along the cliffs
  And silent in the combe
Where walls of blackthorn shut us
  Into a painted room?

O say not we are old,
  Count not our love in years,
We who have counted only
  Love's heartbeats and love's tears.
Time cannot mark our seasons
  Of joy past reasoning;
If Winter is to be apart,
  Together it is Spring!

Mabel V. Irvine

VELVET

HAVE you seen my lady
 Riding through the town,
Clad in moss-green velvet,
 On her pony brown?

Have you seen my lady
 Walking through the street,
Velvet dress and little velvet
 Shoes upon her feet?

Have you seen my lady,
 On an afternoon,
Dressed in vieux-rose velvet
 And vieux-rose velvet shoon?

Have you seen my lady,
 Straight and slim and tall,
Clad in old-gold velvet,
 Going to the ball?

I've seen my lady laughing,
 I've seen my lady sad,
Riding, walking, dancing, talking,
But always velvet-clad.

Gloria Rawlinson

THE MOOR-HOUSE

PRAY enter in and glance around;
   If you should care to view
My little house upon the moor,
   The door is wide to you.

I cut the windows, crystal clear,
   From sliding waterfalls;
I dipped a brush into the sky
   To paint the four bare walls.

And once when Keeper Day had gone
   To rest an hour or two,
I stole some stars — you mustn't tell —
   To make this lamp for you.

The kind sun lights my morning fire —
   A faithful riser he —
The moor-wind calls here every day
   To sweep the floor for me.

It's all to let, if you would deign,
   My Lady, to apply;
We want no rent, we ask but love,
   My little house and I.

Hylda C. Cole

IN AUTUMN

COME, walk upon the sands with me.
  The golden sands, the gentle sea
Are like a summer memory.
November is asleep today,
This is her dream. Hush, let us stay
And watch the coloured fantasy—
Like a blue pansy is the bay
Within a silver cup; the hills
Are gathered at its edge in frills
Of lavender; the sea-bird blows
Like the white petals of a rose
Down the still air. Ah, here is set
The stage for dreams—let us forget
The wintry truth, the wind that sighed,
The drifting year, the turning tide!

Mabel V. Irvine

ALL DAY I'VE TOILED

ALL day I've toiled, but not with pain,
   In learning's golden mine;
And now at eventide again
   The moonbeams softly shine.

There is no snow upon the ground,
   No frost on wind or wave;
The south wind blew with gentlest sound
   And broke their icy grave.

'Tis sweet to wander here at night
   To watch the winter die,
With heart as summer sunshine light
   And warm as summer sky.

O may I never lose the peace
   That lulls me gently now,
Though time should change my youthful face,
   And years should shade my brow!

True to myself, and true to all,
   May I be healthful still,
And turn away from passion's call,
   And curb my own wild will.

Emily Jane Bronte

A MEMORY

GREAT-AUNT Sophia — her curl-framed face
    That stooped to meet my kiss —
Recalls her jasmine's scented grace,
    Her rosebud raspberries.

Her garden-beds of blossoms fair
    She bade trim box enclose;
She'd cupboards full of dainties rare
    And lilies tall, in rows.

As special friend I pulled each weed
    And chose the jam for tea,
Great-Aunt Sophia being old indeed
    While I was only three.

To pinks, sweet williams, gilliflowers,
    She gave a loving care;
White currants hung like pearly showers
    When Aunt Sophia was there.

I'm sure she sadly grieved to die
    And leave her flowers all;
She will not harp eternally,
    She was not musical.

But when from life on earth below
    A poor maimed thing has passed,
She'll dearly love to help it grow
    To strength and joy at last.

Hylda C. Cole

THE WAYFARER

I HAVE said farewell to a grey old town
  Where the smoke-drift veiled the sky.
Now I'm off to the hills, so warm and brown,
  While the lazy hours go by.

I'll wait in the sun by a mossy stile
  And smile, as the morning breeze
Whispers its tale of a faery isle
  That it learned from the restless seas.

Perhaps I'll drowse in a meadow cool,
  With my back to a chestnut tall;
Or fill my pipe by a forest pool
  While the soft blue shadows fall.

I'll dip my hands in a dancing stream
  And envy the swallow's flight,
Ere I lay me down for a gypsy's dream
  In the hush of a summer night.

Peter Cliffe

ACKNOWLEDGEMENTS

Our thanks to the Society of Authors as the literary representative of the estate of John Masefield for "Cargoes"; to the Society of Authors as the literary representative of the estate of Rose Fyleman for "Fairy Music" and "The Child Next Door"; to Lutterworth Press for "East and West" by Fay Inchfawn; to Sydney Bell for "The Linnet", "The Little Rath", "The Little Homes" and "Evening in Whitepark Bay"; to Peter Cliffe for "Idyll", "A Song of Bendish", "Home Thoughts", "Dusk" and "The Wayfarer"; to Glynfab John for "The Wishing Well" and to P. Hugh B. Lyon for "The Deserted Garden".